Mere Mortals

Mere Mortals

POEMS BY

Terese Svoboda

The University of Georgia Press

ATHENS AND LONDON

Published by the University of Georgia Press

Athens, Georgia 30602

© 1995 by Terese Svoboda

All rights reserved

Designed by Betty Palmer McDaniel

Set in 10/13 Sabon

by Tseng Information Systems, Inc.

Printed and bound by Thomson-Shore, Inc.

The paper in this book meets the guidelines for
permanence and durability of the Committee on
Production Guidelines for Book Longevity of the
Council on Library Resources.

Printed in the United States of America

99 98 97 96 95   P   5 4 3 2 1

Library of Congress Cataloging in Publication Data

Svoboda, Terese.
Mere mortals : poems / by Terese Svoboda.
p.   cm.
ISBN 0-8203-1710-1 (pbk. : alk. paper)
I. Title.
PS3569.V6M47   1995
811'.54—dc20   94-29146

British Library Cataloging in Publication Data available

God becomes God when the animals say: God.
                                          —*Johannes Eckhardt*

Acknowledgments

The author and publisher gratefully acknowledge the following publications in which these poems first appeared:

After the Storm, Maisonneuve Press: "Ajax' Mother"
Agni: "A Few Drops of Blood or Grenadine," "Like a Dog, He Hunts in Dreams"
American Poetry Review: "Brassiere: Prison or Showcase?" "Dog/God," "Lithium"
Columbia: "On That Day"
Georgia Review: "A Moo on a Can with a Cow on It"
Gettysburg Review: "A Scarlet Bird"
Hawaii Review: "Epithalamion," "Mother's Minotaur"
Kenyon Review: "The Quick Cave," "The Septic Conversation," "The Smell of Burning Pennies"
The Nation: "Picnic"
Massachusetts Review: "Fairies"
New Yorker: "The Root of Father Is Fat"
Paris Review: "A Cure for Hiccups," "Inventor"
Pequod: "Death for Franchise," "Donkey," "I Kissed Thee Ere I Killed Thee"
Ploughshares: "All Happy Families," "Obscenity," "Philomela"
Prairie Schooner: "Rogue Transmissions," "Sex"
Salamagundi: "Unicorn"
Shenandoah: "The Goddess Corn Finds Her Dress in Disarray"
Southern Review: "To Autumn," "Left-handed Women"
Verse: "Horse's Hooves," "Wait"
Virginia Quarterly Review: "Baiyer River, Papua New Guinea," "Sudanese Civil Sonnet"

Much thanks to Robert Levy and Nancy Shoenberger for their insight and wit, Amy Hempel for her faith, and Mary Stewart Hammond for her extraordinary kindness.

I also enjoyed a residency at Yaddo while working on some of these poems.

Contents

One

Donkey

It takes half a man's life to walk this desert.
Our caravan, though not camelled, proceeds
toward the sun as if it were oasis, though only gears
turn, faint evidence on this flatness

we're moving. We're thankful when women
rail the truck with sticks to create an ambience
of foreignness, and when their men pass
with an armload of corpse, we upend

our knapsacks, we take pictures. For this,
the women put down their sticks and start
an ululation that lifts the scalp a little,
it's that sonorous. As we grind on, the funeral

falls behind: catafalque, pewter, mud bricks,
until the sun aslant doesn't so much allow a last snap
as prevent it. Then a man, down on all fours on top
of a dune, throws back his head and brays so profoundly

we spill our Cokes and say sorry, sorry.

Horse's Hooves

Maman put transistors into circuits
when I am small and playing cook at noon
in the trash behind where she work, the cats
up the casuarina, and Maria with the only spoon,
and the *jefe* gallops from the canebrake
on his gray-spotted mare that later he
poisoned she was so nervous, now the stake
still hanging off her, its wide noose empty
when she jump. At three I am no big thing,
less in a nightie, just more black trouble
in a heap of it. The hooves, they lightning
over, maybe they touch me, but no quarrel
there—just my eyes—Maria screamed Izzie!
then I can't see. Nothing, until I'm nine.
Then Granmere say Okay, look, I busy
with the next baby, so I do. Maman,
she did swear.

                              So when I have a husband
I say I seen these hooves you don't frown now,
and he knowed what I mean. And when I land
at JFK finally, I run down
the stairs like bees was after me because
my sight come back even better when they
give out the nuts and beer. What I seen was
a ghostship—it's a fact—sure as day,
the black struts dangling like a man's two balls,
the Dominican faces all drain white.
And I seen wet red lights down a dark hall.
Sister Maria she too seen lights
but no voices. Izzie, they say, save us,
then groans like they was praying to Santos.

So getting off I tell what I just seen
but the cops don't even bother to phone
after the plane take off and break fifteen
different places. I tell you now, for none
of it matters, and all. See, I have this picture
of two kids. I see the black meeting white,
the broken up dots in the newspaper
all come together, sure as the big fight
in the back of Maman's take-home lighters
that don't need plugs, sure as the old caveman
come out of his cave, looking for his Cain.
I'll be this nanny, and shove the stroller
under a limo. Oh, keep me from it!
I hear that horse, I already done it.
Then you, my last littlest, you go save it
and get crushed to the other, like two magnets.

Baiyer River, Papua New Guinea

The road stops, not in a suburban cul-de-sac
but where the bulldozer's sunk.
Thirty or so men mill at the wreck

in shorts and Coke or Sony T-shirts.
They all have shoes and guns. Dirt
from the "plantesin" seams their skin. The Hertz

rent-a-jeep is theirs, as far as we're
concerned. Last year a missionary, in terror
or bravado, ran a roadblock and disappeared,

and he brought immortality
to the valley—penicillin—which is why
the road got this far, the only

reason. Soon-to-be-extinct butterflies
flutter in pools of urine by
the roadside where they strategize—

for us, for anyone. The road must pay.
Two men wear grass skirts, try to say
our names, as the rest do not. Are they

less hostile because we're their dinner?
To eat means to exploit to all consumers.
Beyond the misty range before

us, gold-capped mountains alchemize
men wearing neckties and Levi's
into Cortez, astride big machines.

Meanwhile,
because it is always meanwhile
back at the pass for someone, all

these night-of-the-living-dead men strip
the jeep, even take the contract and rip
it up for rolling paper, which is when the *If*

this, then—hits home. Why us?
Our T-shirts spell out outrageousness
in their blankness.

We take off the shirts.
If it's not their road, whose
is it? And why so dangerous?

Obscenity

Obscenity is often not an expression
uttered by an individual under great
stress and condemned as bad taste,
but one permitted and even prescribed
by society.
> —*E. E. Evans-Pritchard,*
> British social anthropologist, 1925

Among the Ba-Ila
("among" as if swarming
the petri dish of the British
Imperialist,)

there exist expressions used collectively,
that is, in the presence
of women and children,
in fact, in chorus

since these obscenities
are sung, not scrawled
across a riverbank
where innocent boaters

of Victorian persuasion
might encounter them.
"His great penis is a size!
A thing without end!

It must have a long unwinding!"
The female mourner's song,
the trot arch as if the words
themselves might make

8

the gored warrior rise in tumescence.
Sometimes it's just what they do
with their hands, singing,
writes the patrician scientist

who considered obscenity
a privilege, a way to spur
routine labor with ardor,
or to invoke life

at the moment of death. I drag in
the anthropological so one can reject
the paradigm of the primitive,
we who have no physical labor

which requires our neighbor,
nor sustained interest in creation—
except in art, that work
to ward off death.

There will always be those
in the boat who slow down,
who listen and transcribe
in their tiny script.

Sudanese Civil Sonnet

12,000 Sudanese boys
walked across 600 miles to
Kenya—and back, when no
one offered refuge.
      —New York Times, 1990

The bones scatter not as impressively
as the elephants', unless you call it
a decorator's statement, massed thousands
for color and texture. Lots of texture
here, especially where the bones complicate
with smaller sets. Still, Mathew Brady would
have tossed in some rifles for effect.

The CNN staff doesn't bother. They
whirr overhead where it's cooler, uncowed
by the close cruising Hueys. This war's cheap,
it uses no bullets, eating's the only
political statement. Why, these bones
could be theirs, so white, so strong, so recent.

The Quick Cave

"No hobos here, just homeless—"
the grease monkey pulls a face when I ask
about the turnoff.
                    Where the map says left
at the hobo shack

                    is culvert,
the cave entrance gone
            like the inked-in oval
                    of a cartoon duck.
Rutting skunks

                skitter past my fender,
        and peepers shrill at my paced-out
hundred yards closer. Spring,
            with all its transparent
flatulence, or fall,

when nothing's glamorously
green, is best for spelunking—
            if there's light.
            I whack
            at the moss for loose rocks.

                    A murderers' lair it was,
        no seducers' hideaway, a saucer
of spit tobacco, flies stuck
            on tallow, the harsh breath
of two men in sortie.

Or so I think.
The dog skinnies to where two rocks
lean, whining so I understand
    underfoot's a world, as above,
squirrels change trees.

    Psychopaths we'd call them now—
        then, legend: one Indian killer,
one Indian who killed. Consider the Vietcong,
    and the Ho-Ho who run the restaurant in town,
and how the vet chooses daily between them.

    Quick's father,
fishing on ice in winter,
was killed by the Delaware,
    his blood starring the surface
all season,

    his son driven mad
        by the deer licking the salt
from it—and the thaw,
    when thick red chunks spun
on rapids for an hour.

    Cahounzie was kidnapped by trappers,
taken to England to be turned into traitor,
    a translator. But the moment
the boat came back, he fled
    to woods so much the same

    after ten years, his hatchet
lay in its proper hollow. But his people,
    apropos a film's creaking coincidence,
lay dead in their smoking huts, dead
    by the Delaware.

Now in neither tale does anyone ask
        who died on the Delaware side,
                whose real estate was on the line,
        as true vengeance must first be washed
                in innocence.

        Remember TV's blood-curdling howls?
At Eagle's Nest, above the truck stop,
        the two made an oven
        out of natural stone pillars
                then pushed

one red-hot boulder over,
        a kind of bowling with fire,
                and it lit the cliff and crushed
thirty Delaware fishing
        at the river.

You can still find their arrows,
        and eagles hover there,
                chromosomes remembering carrion.
        I guess Quick died in bed,
and not in the cave,

        and Cahounzie,
crazed after the hot rock debacle
        (too much the same as his own homecoming),
                married an Astor. What does it
        matter? A pink "2" is painted

on a granite outcrop—State Fish and Game's
        memorial? It's still no clue.
                I can't find the cave.
        All I know is that trains run past,
                like they do all the dark venues.

A Few Drops of Blood or Grenadine

If not rain, then sleet. North
of the equator by several boundaries,
the beach a swill in rainbowed oil
sixty stories down, he drinks
something slick traced with pink,
matching both the slurried sunset
and what's washing up. I'm late,
arriving. The bar begins revolving.
An exile, he starts, does not take
an airline to her mother's.

It is a state, I suggest. Always.
A wall falls and still we're pressing.
I am the daughter exchanged for cattle:
wife, the oldest outcast. The airline
is my mother: Ta-ta! she waves
at the open hatchway. To that,
he orders another round. If love
chafes, then cut it, cut it,
cut it. You're not bitter enough.
I'm sorry. You're not sorry enough.

O.K. The exile's invisible, that trope.
You ask for peasant sapphics—listen
to that piped-in dreck. You think
slaves turn this bar, stories down?
They're on the street, palms out.
One man does not a ripple make,
in hopeless love, in clichéd country.
He squints: Ah, all she wants is
an out-of-the-body funk under palms
and some swimming pool of desire

she's too young to die in.
As for silence, her language condones it,
the "e" on the end of "exile." He coughs
the name Kurz over the last sweet drink
and it could be the capital of any
overly developed country, the beach below
opening its sores as the stinking wind
rakes it. But we are nearly home,
the circles closing on those who watch,
blind guilt revolving, from here
instead of there, dissembling.

Two

Faust

Prologue

Born again in the bosom of our Lord
in a tent in Tennessee and not for
the first time, Faust—dazed in Asia Minor,
sated in a Benedictine abbey,
bodiless inside a dead volcano,
flipped out on the slick black infinity
of a speedway, not to mention speed—seeks
experience, not knowledge, not the on-
off of a machine with chips for innards,
nor the drub genius's recital for
a game show now fallen out of favor.
She wants to be the whole race, the jockey
and the bettor, the horse too. (In Bali
she witnessed four boys in a trance canter
like Percheron.) But Faust, at thirty-eight,
is tired, ensconced on a beach, its harbor
filled with freighters packed with sonar beepers
and armored vehicles—the medieval
setup of the Known World—not the Third,
on which she sits, sans innocence. She's known
death's the reward for both sin and virtue
since her grad school years as a magician's
assistant, the woman in sequins who
tries to distract you from whatever end
is being conjured yet you still yearn for.
Now she turns armored vehicles to scrap
and back, for money. The beaten ploughshare
and the rest, just another transaction
over the phone or fax. What's left is her,

and what happens, which is why she's here
and not in some plastic Known World office.
It's all that Other—how, like a goat sniffing
a cartoon can, she is greedy for it.

It's so bright Faust keeps her shades on
through breakfast, which she takes alone and likes.
While the ocean creeps umbrellas closer,
and the fowl ducks the bread chunks she tosses
from the empty table beside her, men
and boys hawk their Chiclet baggage, belts from
Hong Kong, gummy instant snaps, lewd statues
in forced perspective. A boy in three plaids,

Plaid, and another wearing a hostile T-shirt,
"Be Bad" with a dictator's picture screened
across it, pluck at her sleeve. *Mi amor,*
Gesundheit—the accent matches anything
she offers. What they want is their own four
seconds under a multinational's
arches—but that they don't tell her, posing
her with T-Shirt. She buys the Polaroid,
which she hands to Plaid. You're very blatant,
she laughs. Still, she buys it.

Plaid dribbles lotion down Faust's topless back,
her bare nipples flat to the beach towel
and thus modest, about as subtle
a maneuver as the blimp swinging
over them. With a wave of wet pinkie,
he suggests in patois as polyglot
as his much-invaded heritage,
a trip to his place. She winds the towel
around her bust, flips over, whispers, Well . . .

Despite the surf, T-Shirt makes out
the gist of Plaid's intent and is brushing
the sand off himself when she finishes:

       Black mass, voodoo, sissi, conjure—you know—
for the same money.

            She's old anyway.
Why not, Plaid shrugs, forgetting and using
his TV accent, that lingo lip-synched
by everyone in satellite-Babel.

While she dresses, T-Shirt paces.

Let's rip

her off, leave what's left to the gulls. Who needs
her grinning like she's on to us?

Plaid's not sure.

From the labels I see on her luggage
she could foot college, depending on how
abuen we got her.

The crone down the beach

selling Coke mutters:

Look at those *selgros,*

probably dealing drugs like the poor man
now zigzagging over the greased prone bodies
with the *guardia* after him, firing
at the ocean to avoid sunbathers
and hitting native swimmers. And when I
call a taxi to take the sooner-or-
later-bleeding dealer to his instant
trial, they'll divide the take like pirates,
one-half to the maid who did the tip-off.
Sell their souls? The vendor clucks. The question
is how often, how much, what location.

Act II, Scene 1

While Plaid scatters the usual kids-in-
attendance, T-Shirt collects her hundred
and changes it, most of it laid on one
Tony Le Tour whose blurred perimeter
and omnibus grin suggest any well-
greased request gets serviced.

                    Sess this, honey,
This be no barbecue. Black mass, they go
pricey. He produces the wallet he's lifted
from her, then kisses it. I'll take credit
for the rest, he offers, then impresses
her imprint onto three carbons. She squawks,
but weakly. The more risk costs, the better.

Catching the drift, Plaid and T-Shirt retreat
to Tony's where they work on Mastermind
in his parlor. Right away the icon
from the game starts saying interesting things—
not just Nuke 'Em—to wit: overthrow fueled
by hate based on per pixel of skin tone
occuring on-screen. The strangest thing is
it doesn't beg more change. Even when Plaid
slops Fanta over the controls, which makes
the joystick stick good, it keeps on playing.
They don't get it, banging Free Game, Free Game,
all that one economy indentured
to another calls for, and thus they miss
the message, specifically the Hell it
previews for them so cheaply in color,
the circuitry and plastics smoldering.

                    *   *   *

Meanwhile, Tony's cut Faust's thumb to drip blood
over a brazier where white coals sizzle.
He won't join veins or deal with needles.

                                                    AIDS
be a dumb monkey to get on your back,
he says.
            Better be good, she breathes into
her tube top, squeamishly. I've seen Thailand,
crept into the Sphinx's belly, done most
of Bali.
            Don't wail so, girlie. See—smoke.
That we got for the dog-stuck-with-cock dance,
a kind of shivaree they get into
after a horse mounts a man as he flays
monkeys whose skulls be opened for you to
scoop out the brains of. Entrails go extra.

Her beach towel hisses in kerosene flame.

            Good, she says, I go for it.
                                    Tony taps
his Ray-Bans on the dark lens part where she's
reflected against the fire.

                        This be good,
he chuckles.
            Then she sees fire, a writhing torso,
and—
        laughs.

            Why, it's Marlowe. Nice to see
you. She turns to face him.

                      Blind in one eye,
with a twisted grin that keeps the other
open, he nods.

                  Still in development?

It's the devil's business.

                    Marlowe stomps out
the embers while Tony exits with two
well-done chickens.

                  They buss. My dear, you—

Palms rustle, split. Plaid hands her her car keys.

                Thanks for all this, she murmurs. Do take care.

Sounds like a warning, Ma'm, he says. Then he
clears out quick, as Marlowe, in the shadows,
frisbees his Elizabethan collar
into the bush.

                So what's the deal, Faust? Like:
Had I as many souls as there be stars
I'd give them all to you? Love the beat.

                Christ, she breathes.

Please. Marlowe raises his hand.
                      Watch your tongue.
He parts more palms. Look over here.

Two teams
under torchlight volley a human head.
One player waggles hello with his tail.

Jesus.

Hey, says Marlowe, I mean it, keep it down.

She whispers: You had a condo in Rome
when we last . . .
her voice trails off.

In *People*
I'm the devil himself—and I quote.

Sure.

I'm what you paid for.

No. She claps her hand
to her mouth. Oh, no. Not you. And besides,
The only soul I have is on CD.

My dear Faust, please do try to rise above
bad material. Now, who could this be?

The underbrush springs opens again for
seven tourists plus Tony who traipse through
the clearing, all but him hung with cameras.

A real deadly bunch, he says *in sotto*,
I had to do something—they was driving
me over. Now I know you thought you was
paying for a private thing—

                        She slaps him,
then turns on his brood. Who are you?

                                    Name tags
rustle. A three-piece safari-clad shark
steps up, clears his throat and mumbles, Credit,
number one of the more Deadly Sins. He's
followed by the Boredoms from Akron who
curtsy, all three of them. Then the couple
in back—Sex and Violence—her breasts shoot
condoms, his crotch drops grenades, muscle up.
            We're in case she gets antsy with this shit.

Sex twists toward the Jewish American Princess
who whines she does not want to be waited on
but to get their asses back on the bus
because her feet hurt.

                        It's souvenirs they've
come for: the knotted rag, dyed hen feathers,
misshapen wedges of rubber. Laden,
they can-can off.

                        Tomorrow, says Tony,
winking at Sex, I'll take you all further.
Then, passing Faust, he asks after Marlowe.
Kickbacks, you know.

                        But he's gone and no one
knows where, not even T-Shirt who's flat
on his back in the bush still up from the stuff
he found in her purse, hallucinating.

That Marlowe's a clever dude. Look, he's left
the rubber and the spoon. I wonder—
says Plaid.

    T-Shirt leans over their trash can
and vomits.

    You're messing me up, Plaid shrieks.

   I'm thinking of her, Ms. Beach Bitch.
         Shirt jacks
up his shorts. She wants us.

       And she makes you
sick? Plaid can't control his shaking.

   This is different. I drank six Classic Cokes
with a whistle of bay rum out at Dan's
Food Locker. I'm getting pure like angels.

   Well, hell, grow wings.
        Plaid needles his forearm
for a clean stretch of unexploited skin.
I'm good. All I need is to get wasted.

Act III

She's enhammocked and the stars have broken
into mirrors with one of her in each, stretched
palm to palm, swaying and wondering
where would the center of experience
lie now that Marlowe will provide it, if
and when he signs off on her numerous
addenda to the contract, those being:
that Faust go invisible whenever,
that Marlowe be her slave regardless,
that he should not bore her with his conquests.
For this he gets her soul when it's ready,
the appropriate moment, *la belle morte,*
when she figures she won't mind anyway.

      I'll hook onto some bigger wheel then,
like air or dirt maybe. Death's a dull devil
really. Besides, there's always repentance.
And how can hell be so bad—look around—
this is, after all, the middle class, Sartre-
soaked with loss of meaning, and burnt alive
by the ozone sky that holds its heaven.

      Tempus fugit, Baby, reads Marlowe off
the tattoo appearing on her tricep.
Time will fly.

Act III, Scene l

All bad women die at the end of films,
the good ones die earlier. Marlowe hands
her the deconstructed airplane dinner
and winks his good right eye.

                The clouds outside
glancing off the plane turn into Trigger,
King Kong, then Zsa Zsa's top half.

                  If it's badness
you're after,

          he saws at the blue plastic
covering his butter,

              then L.A.'s the place.
"Lost Angels," a major center, hometown
to so many of us, the smog simply
Hell's signature. If you make it there—
Marlowe's eyebrows rise.

            Skip the soaps, sitcoms,
franchises—what I want is an Oscar.
Faust jerks salt over her chicken.

              He laughs.
A pot metal man? The silver peeling
from his prayerful hands in twenty-five years,
the tape disintegrating, Faust who? in five?

       If I live after I'm gone, what good
does it do me? Forget this immortal
shit—this is the twentieth century.
I want applause, a standing ovation—
the homage of crowds awed at my cleavage.

Marlowe laughs again.
One must not be so
limited. I control the stuff of kid's
Saturday mornings. With me, just your voice
could send them straight to the psychiatrist's.

Well, a little immortality can't
hurt. But I don't have to be bad. Faust picks.
A decent, not too literate script—

Marlowe hesitates, scribbling pentagrams
on his napkin. You'll need a good costar,
a Christmas release date. And what about
public opinion? I mean, even for
talking fridges, they've got ratings.
Faust yawns.
You fix it.

*   *   *

The red limo glides between palms to
an East Coast fantasy of indolence
which paradoxically suggests power,
its exhaust fueling a dry-ice rapture,
a special with naiads of all ages
and costume *en fin,* though through the smoked glass
there's little nuance.

Let's cruise on over
to Betty's. I've read all about Betty,
says Faust through the speaker. Lynch has lunch with
Betty.
Marlowe cringes. At least she's not
insisting we channel.

*   *   *

Betty's perched on
her gardener when Marlowe makes it over.

No time for stools—besides, I'm not heavy,
right, Borges?
The man's wearing glasses
so thick you can't tell if he's sleeping, crouched
on his knees, head to hands.

What's this, Marlowe?
Sam's signing who instead of my client?
This babe's got zilch but he's going for it.
Step up, take a peep through the fence.
You can see him nodding—or is Sho-Tu
just doing shiatsu across his fat neck?

Betty stomps twice, barely missing Borges's
tailbone.
The butler's coming with Chivas
on silverplate. Why can't he tell *schniffzers*
when they all but do it in front of him?

She's an actress, Marlowe chuckles.

Betty's
not amused. She almost falls off her stool
but for its one arm up.

We want costars,
Marlowe orders suddenly.

Betty's eyes
widen. She's yours? I don't believe it. Her?
Okay, she grumbles. For you, I'll get. But
she's no moneymaker. She'll be bored by
the time the press kit's out—she'll see she can't

play every part, that life's too short, even
hers. And—Betty narrows her eyes—
the screens are getting smaller, the tape
deals aren't so hot anymore, the public
doesn't like women getting the good parts
unless they're in love with the hero—she'll
have to have a hero.

So? says Marlowe.
Thank god Shakespeare's not around.

Yes, the stage.
She'll do Cleveland, cries Betty. How perfect.

Marlowe frowns. So what's left on your contract?

Betty shivers.
Let's renegotiate.

Sweetheart, we are. He gives her a sort of
special smile.
Then he shouts Bugs! and unplugs
three of them fixed to the gardener's headset.

Naturally. I'm organic, says Betty.

But Borges weeps:
My front page with the *Star*!
I hate trimming Douglas fir and doing
Betty every Sunday. This was to be
my big break.

You can do me Saturdays!
cries Betty.

At which point the Chivas bursts
into flame as Sam toasts Faust exiting.

Plaid and T-Shirt lurk under an awning.
So what if I have his green card, says Plaid.
Yeah, says Shirt. And if this punk geek thinks
he can hassle us—
              They hunker themselves
into their leather as a Vietnamese
hood storms over.
                 Look, it takes much trouble
to run these cards. I have plenty guns to
get them back.
             Hey, Khemosabi, says Plaid,
Who's got cards?
              Why would we want them? We're just
tourists. T-Shirt turns his pants pockets out.
The hood grabs Plaid by the nape and shakes him.
Plaid shouts Valet! and pulls out a twenty,
nodding toward the awning's cafe. Get him.

In minutes, Marlowe, napkin still tucked in,
bangs through the double glass doors. You deadheads!
The Oriental backs off with bows, So
sorry, while Marlowe sputters: May you both
stay wetbacks—grease monkey and car collie—
and chase Audis all day in Kmart lots.
I'm under contract to Faust, not you dopes.

Act IV

The White House whitens every dawn with pure
intention as men from the cleaning staff
repack their vans and venture forth onto
the thickening beltway. Marlowe points this out
as their shuttle circles, and about how
the bright monuments refuse to mirror
the decayed sprawl of abandoned suburbs
so like, philosophically, the feudal
that where power beads the streets in swarms of
motorcades, the empty lanes seem runways
for certain Renaissance angels.

Really?
      Frank from maintenance scratches skin
best left to the ravages of soda
and chocolate.
           Oscar, the underling,
carrying the Xeroxes and out of breath,
nods his head again.
               Yeah, they said just to
put the time in for her—rock stars, even
Elvis, wait years. But she swears she can get
Lincoln on the line. Remember the prime
minister from Canada who ran things
consulting monkeys?

      So what? mutters Frank.
We had seancing twice last term. Uh-oh—
Ben.

      Yo! The newsman slaps Oscar's behind.
How come no invite to this circus? What
happened to freedom of the press? I'll raise
hell if I'm not given a pass. I can't
stand courtroom sketches, let alone hearsay.
Why, without TV, who'd take the head
honcho's word for it? Half the U.S. didn't
believe Nam existed until it played
Huntley-Brinkley.

           Hush, try 104B.
Oscar hands him the magnetic key. But
don't let Faust see you. She's the one who wants
it secret.
      Ben nods, notes, buzzes for freight.
The things I do. I'll bet my belly tuck
she's not such hot stuff.

Act IV, Scene 2

The president puts his feet precisely
where P.R. steps—to make his shoulders sway.
(They think it helps his image.) Behind him,
the first lady in official drag chats
up Ms. Faust whose shoulders sway naturally,
and whose costume vies Cher's taste in show biz,
a kind of sensual smokescreen of net
and well-placed sequins, surefire as any she
had as an assistant to distract them.
Marlowe's last in the named entourage,
the others following are CIA,
by business invisible, and Borges,
who still seems to see nothing.

                                    They enter
the redecorated rear ballroom which
opens on itself like a postmodern
Babylonian brothel, in view of
a certain bathroom window. There Faust stops,
gathers her tattered libidinous cape
and fires its accessory rockets
to provide the necessary splendor
and more smoke. Then she taps Marlowe who has
Lincoln enter, sign a few autographs
and wave to the black janitor. When he
begins to rave about his nutsy wife,
how the bios are always wrong, and runs
over to the president to shake hands,
Faust decides to tune him out, or, rather,
Marlowe.

        The brass love it. With hot V.R.
like that, we could project carnage over

any major region with real detail,
enough to convince the U.N. to let
us go in and protect our interests—
regardless.

You see now why I didn't
want the press. Faust smiles until she tips
back on her heels and sees Ben, his newsman's
belly overhanging the window box
on 104. Madam, says Ben, tugging
at his shirtfront, it is really myself
and the forces behind me who have made
you what you are today.
Nonsense, she says,
and grins at Marlowe.

I'll expose her, swears Ben. I've got
guys in malls, in airport check-in, captains-
of-the-bellhops galore. Every limo
that drives the park, windows dark, antenna up—
they'll check the plates, even the plastic skin
on the roof outlined in chrome, and catch her.

          We got her already, walkies Oscar.
They snap on the lights.

               Experience, she's
telling Marlowe who's half-dozing,
                      doesn't
equal knowledge, for experience is
known and the other remains a matter
for conjecture—scientists are always
telling us the facts, then taking them back—
and there's that fleet smile of the announcer
when he gives us the news like it's the truth.
Marlowe, listen. You don't need sleep. And look,
the light's changing.

          Photographers flash at
the windows. Too bad for them, Marlowe's loaned
her an infrared cloak to snuggle in
so they get nothing.

Act IV, Scene 4

Out of malls and airport check-ins march men
with matching overarching potbellies,
angry with Ben that their women make
fun of them, and in a profession
so riddled with personal appearance
fetishes, even behind the cameras,
they're sure they're jinxed for further advancement.
But Ben especially, bouncing as he takes
the stairs to editorial, for all
he has to show is receipts for coffee.

Marlowe, ain't you got love in there? Let's see
love. Or is love too afflatus for you
who works the whole universe? Come on, Marl,
put out.
             Sighing, he gives her a profile
of a member so tenderly pressing
a zipper she nearly misses it.
                          So,
I don't do it for you. Well, let's review,
in crudité, what you prefer.
                    Out of
air just as thin as anywhere appear
two yearlings at rest in quite intimate
poses on the divan.
                Historically,
Faust commands. Winners of past pageants slink
through the bedroom in flesh tights and jockstraps.
She sighs. Marlowe, I'm surprised. I thought talk
counted for something.

                   My Lustwaffe, that's me.
He puts her hand against his throat, then moves it
to the aforementioned spot on his front.
Feel how they are the same? When the spirit's
on them—he cocks his head toward the lounging,
muscled display—they too will talk. Even
Helen had to hear something. But the real
art in seduction is more like TV's—
it's not what you say. To demonstrate he
snaps on the set and all turn right to it.

Okay, she says, what about me? I'd like
my own prime specimens, the chest that stopped

a thousand bullets, the head that merged two,
no, three nations, or packaged movie deals
with major players.
                    Then have him fall to?
Marlowe laughs. I think I love you.

            So do.

                    The men vanish into their air.
One thing, Faust whispers, you won't knock me up?

            Hey, Marlowe breathes into her nethers, we
could unmake the world like this, if you wish.

My dear, I'd like something genuine
I can auction later at Sotheby's,
something late but permanent, tasteful
but not irreproachable.
      The hag, all
Yves Saint-Laurent down to her shimmery
hosiery, shakes her shopping gear in case
Faust doesn't get the gist. She's from her past.

Faust flings open her closet, chooses a skirt
of serviceable plush and the woman
grovels, as if grateful.
      Don't ever let
perfume touch it, Faust warns.
      Oh, I'd never,
she returns, I'll mark the label. But just
a few minutes later, in the foyer,
she unhooks it from the hanger, slithers
into it and goes for the atomizer.
I'll walk through a squirt in suspension
de toilette—it's like cigarette smoke,
for godsake, and my lover will love it.
She squirts.

     Faust lies fast asleep, knees to chin,
gray roots exposed. The woman with her bags
returns, creeps to the bedside, the skirt
a stinky stiff insert from *Glamour,*
no line anymore to speak of, nothing
even a good dry cleaner can salvage.
Pearls alone light the room, the plum-sized strand
on Faust's neck that pulses in soft flesh tones.
These the crone slides off, clasps to herself. Pop!
The pearls start oozing fat in big white gobs.

Blanc du blanc grapes, peeled, are fruit's *force majeure*
rolled in whipped cream and baked. I read about
them in *Gourmet*, the Eurotrash woman
with connections in hyphens relates. And
they're never out of season. Her husband
nods, perhaps a duke in businessman's garb.

     Faust rebukes: Have you ever had a Real
Tomato? Even Holland can't import
the warm, thin-skinned type that's as sweet and slick
as sex, an endangered species so rare
the stomach actually sits up and smiles.

     Ah, sighs the Mrs., ah, ah. Faust conjures
two beefsteaks, *eau de la coeur*, poison-red.
The man groans with a bass Texas rumble
learned late in discos, and she too, the O
poised on her lips like a runway model's.

     Just then Plaid, T-Shirt and the em-pearled woman
clap under the posh restaurant's false archway
and Plaid steps forward into a klieg light
with a threatening:
               Devil—

               Whereupon
Faust freeze-frames him. Then T-Shirt rushes her
but Faust gets him too, without bothering
with the controller, then the woman starts,
then stops.
          The maître d' smiles, hands folded.
Yet Faust allows them their mission *à la*
slow motion, one syllable at a time.
The result is sonorous, plangent and

Fascinating, as the duchess—if he's
really a duke—says *in sotto* with How
I'd love that on my console. What about
instant replay?

Faust laughs long, embittered.
Stick to memory. It's primitive but
time-tested, heaven if you're any good
at blocking the unsavory. Even
I have used it.

The Duke takes her hand.
By golly, you're our favorite. Sommelier!
But the stains streaking his tie at the end
of the meal are all fresh tomato.

Plaid's at watch on the curb in an old coat,
used to the chill by now, no island boy
in the wrong world. An occasional bus
full of rubbernecks pass, and then one stops,
empties its contents to stare at Faust's house,
led by Borges.
              Life's just done a spread on
the most desirable male of all time
and it's—one old lady pirouettes—
Schwarzenegger! We want him now!
                                Borges
urges them on in a frenzied chanting.

Faust obliges, sending out pure flexing
male beauty.
            But he's dead, one of them shouts,
like all our husbands.
                     What about Ms. Faust?
She's dead too.

             Faust reaches through the window
with one long-clawed finger, and rebukes:
After Eve, all women were fallen and
thought not worth temptation. I've changed all that.
And I still have my man.

                 She draws him past
the mostly old widows *en flagrante*.

We want regrets, they shout. Regrets. Regrets.

At this, Faust slams the window shut so hard
the beefcake's left outside as afterthought

which vanishes like hot breath on a pane.
Later, Plaid scans the security tapes
in a back bedroom half asleep and notes
that each of the *kvetching* women leaves
with her face smeared with Innocence, a cream
of Faust's peddled at the souvenir shop.

A sequinned threesome sings *Too Bad, So Sad,*
to a downbeat from a box, the lights dim
where half-shut eyes, bare backs mingle, hors d'oeuvres
and drinks in hand.

     A spotlight announces
Faust, doyenne, who takes a seat on a throne,
just back from hang gliding over Borneo.
A trip, she says and no more.

       Marlowe wafts
in behind her. When the lights start to strobe,
his good eye glows bright behind his black shades.

Dis is dat, croons Borges in blackface, *What
a woman knows.* The spot finds the chorus,
six in tails and forks.

     Dis is dat, they groan,
in rare unison.

      * * *

     Cocktails over now,
Faust redresses, tries earrings, removes them.

Why not the amethyst? Carol offers
two eye-level.

    Or opal—this is Tina,
a sweet first communicant from Jersey.
I'm afraid Cartier's is closed.

      So what?
Faust fondles the guard, opens it, locates
the crowns and puts one on.

                                Repetition
is the key to all experience, she
decrees. Cell on cell, humping, remembering,
brains in lethargy absently butting
synapses for additional meaning.
Knowledge is—

                    Faust stops. Are you listening?
I've been dead wrong. All experience is
is Alzheimer's reversed. Get it?

                            It's eleven
whispers Tina.
                        How do you know? Faust steps
behind her as if the clock were watching.
Then she laughs, then she stops again.
                                        Marlowe
once said, Fools who laugh on earth, weep in—

Carol clears her throat.

                        Faust wails: It's meaning
I miss, the translation. What's all this mean?

                        Tina skitters up,
                        Take this. She presses
a pill to Faust's lips.

                        Experience, Faust
hisses, throwing it down. The whole of life,
this cup that can't be taken away or
taken over. But, maybe—
                            She shivers.

                            50

                                  My forehead
shavings—they're frozen? The egg's
in saline solution? The sweet agar-
agar's clotted with genes up the whazoo?
Science is God, I tell you. I'll see Him
soon.

        The maids fade,
                        saying, We'll make a request—
something you like, a frenzied lambada.

                        That's not me—don't you know me?
The real me? Faust taps one silicone breast
as if it would soften. Experience
is like what backs money. We spend our life,
secure there's gold behind it.
                                Or something.

They don't even know me.
                        She unlocks drawers
and she finds the doll that Tony le Tour
gave her at that long-ago beachside toot.
This she now unpierces, watching each hole
as it leaks out its terrible fine soot.

Act V, Scene 3

You heard what? The coroner asks, taping
the doors closed.

                    Nothing.
                              Plaid denies, denies,
denies. And my buddy T-Shirt heard zip
too. Ask that other guy, Marlowe.

                                        First name?

Chris, I guess. But he's checked out with the rest.
Plaid buttons his coat a little higher.
What gives?

                        She seems to have gone to pieces.
The coroner holds up three full baggies
labeled liver.
                    Any children?

                              Plaid scuffs
at the carpet, its Persian möbius
making him dizzy.

                        How could she, of all
people, have skipped having children?

                                        Hey. Plaid
tosses the key to her memoirs into
a vent. What she knew wouldn't duplicate.

EPILOGUE

By the time Buddha's wheel inches forward
and shows what a good life she lived, that is,
rich from a newsman's p.o.v., she'll be
one with the imploding frozen starlight,
the sucking black hole starting in Marlowe's
bad eye from which you don't return. Beyond
boredom, the twentieth-century hell
of a certain class, she'll have paid the price
of her indulgence. There is no template,
no metal with memory uncoiling
and coiling upon which experience lives.
The sum vanishes. Faust joins Being,
what's left merely electricity.

Three

Like a Dog, He Hunts in Dreams

—Tennyson

The dog-soul, fetus-curled, whirling in space,
eyes closed—from nausea? nirvana?—arrives.
Cerberus, whose three heads menace men only—
hardly the Lassie of the classics,
mostly simpering poodle indicative of
corruption, the least beastly vice,
lowest human—teaches the frozen,
not in any way wagging, dog-soul
not to bark at the shadows that show up.

All the animals shut up alive with Ramses
and the likewise wife, howl.
Their helplessness eased the passage,
as did the dog of our youth, matching
kerchiefs round our necks. The dog
is us, like toys, a commodity to which we bring
self-love. The huge dingo that bore Adam and Eve
from his fur on the other side of the world
rests now, as each fierce Samoyed is eaten
to keep the sled going. Dogs, poets, hunting.

The Goddess Corn Finds Her Dress in Disarray

—with apologies to Herrick

Imagine corn new-discovered, tassels
showing up in fashion, and bucketfuls
of ears gracing fancy dress balls.
Why, to intimate your lover's teeth, all
a-glistening, were like new corn
said much for the seventeenth-century lovelorn.
The goddess on the boxfront
of cornstarch is all that's left of the ancient
American idol
in her accoutrement bridal.

Europeans deny their envy—
let Freud or Lacan explain it. Trotsky
died in corn country but never
rallied to her honor.
'Tis she! 'Tis she! Guns
exploded in unison, Mexican
thugs happy to avenge her lest she be
unreconstructed, the
dialectics of food, like sex
or politics, all interest.

That is, the principal is spent and no
supply exists. To return to the flow
of season whence this aforesaid corn
makes frolic the lark, if you're born
nine months later
perhaps it's allergies that your mother
hid from, naked and quilt-covered,

while in the field for days haze hovered,
storms of propagation
permitting no human reason.

Traditionally fate fills her bucket
and it leaks. Thus: to market, to market,
a pagan harvest of Saffoil
and plastics—what everything boils
down to. Why praise corn,
her seeming assets, when squeezed and shorn,
pregnant women eat and inhale
birth defects, their genes matching the new-failed
kernels zigzagging as crazy
as spray planes over Jersey?

For ashes to ashes, read soap. Last year
she appeared on the Schlitz sign downtown, beer-
cap-crowned, almost Guadalupe
(no tribute to Trotsky)
and entreated civil
disobedience, corn hoarded, the evil
Empire evacuated.
Few did more than honk. She miscalculated,
counting on pure beauty
and our lack of fertility.

Philomela

by the barbarous king
So rudely forced
—Eliot,
The Waste Land

Aunt Phil was no *fin de siècle* brooched-up
elegant with one eye always on the carat,
though she almost married several goose-
bottomed men. I begin where the last
had the balls to jilt her. She'd even
put down a deposit at the engravers, spent
a mint on her teeth when he'd phoned. She pulled
the phone out. She was my mother's sister.

Letting the cost of subsequent long
long distance calls slip by and given her
now advanced age, twenty-five, we invited her
to live with us. Poor Aunt Phil, Mom sighed,
she'd sooner couch-faint than admit
anybody'd hurt her. But she'd already taken
a job at a furriers. Then Dad, on his way
back from a newscast, offered to escort her.

Now Phil had Dad first, before Mom, casting us
in relative shade, but good Phil
moved away, routing this, lest we savage
the soap's adage: out of bitterness, rise
to new bitterness. Villainous as this is,
Dad stopped by anyway, offered his Mileage Plus
upgrade, saying he didn't need it, saying
all was forgiven. Meaning? Phil tapped.

But charmed by his new look, rewoven hair
where before large areas shone bare,
and the tacky plastic mike pinned to his lapel,
she called Mom to say she was coming, no mention
why now. Besides, it was such innocence,
the California palms cushioning takeoff,
the ever-less thirst-quenching Collins,
the overhead compartment popping open. At this point

Mom throws back the headrest on the La-Z-Boy
and I have to work out the rest myself.
Dad had not lived with us for a while. I say this
to exonerate our taste, much as parents do
with small children at table. But this was worse:
Phil and Dad retired to the plane's sole place
of liaison, and somehow in their vertical struggle,
he bit it off, that bulbed folded-over, that area

of interest, and not by accident. When she screamed,
he slipped out, jammed the door shut.
It took four men to unlock her at Newark.
She didn't turn up the day she'd promised,
but we didn't worry. She was Phil, she had her silences.
When Dad came to pick us up for the weekend
he suggested she'd flaked off, driven crazy
by rejection. Phil? She has plenty to choose

from. Mom shook her head. Just some are losers.
Dad sighed, picked at his mike, flashed
first-run tickets. She's just like your mother.
Mom glared, blowing a kiss to me and my brother.
I mention him last because he meant so little
to me, being little. He was born during Dad's
reweaving, during reconstruction, if not peacetime
here. Maybe Phil's going gay, Mom debated,

hearing nothing, or she has AIDS.
We began to worry. Then, in a final bit
of embroidery, Phil faxes Mom the truth,
each pixel in crewel design. Mom kills
my little brother and has Dad over to eat him.
This is almost literal. I mean, both ladies
split, we kids looking too much like Dad,
and it's my brother who understands

less, who draws maps of how to drive home,
who stays in a corner for one whole year
and Dad doesn't tell Mother. No, this is not
a feminist history, nor even a blowup
of the middle class. When Dad acts like a god
on the five o'clock news, all we can do
is turn down the sound and crow like Aunt Phil,
grappling in midair, singing our betrayal.

I Kissed Thee Ere I Killed Thee

—Othello

The moon drops. The sirens clutch their one note.
Night is a lidded pit where our arms
brush neither stars nor soot.
We feel our breasts, the tips rise, alarmed,
as out there some pitched god swaggers, unsheathed
and mewing, the tenor of which turns and stops
her whom our embarrassed coughs only strop
her fascination. She wants to take the napped head
and rub. He unfolds, the skin the sheen of lead

And dismisses her, considering little
the enormity of her ardor, pulps
the fruit with his one godlike stance, the sibyl's
untoward grimace his. Night riddles
her as she climbs his dark limbs
with sex, all its chilling rhythms
shutting off night and day, the usual order
but here night is bigger, the moon's a supernova.

Here a millenia of famine turns to
conflagration until the hoary lean-to
on an African island comes to stand for
all pleasure. A hunger for mirrors
blackens the backs of stars.
She wriggles free, unharmed, a pregnancy
surely. We croon behind her,
a chorusing Pleiades:

What subsumes this? Nothing's
ignored in that vast flat place, the world,
each ridge marks a falling, each sidling
scrabble a break in lovemaking.
Better, who asks this to be? The quiet woman,
the priapic salesman of color? No one
denies the grip of the generative,
the live
jet emptying. The wheat comes up
and it's morning, the sex stopped.

Ajax' Mother

> What is honor?
> A word.
> > —*Falstaff*

Two rivals, Homer tells me,
and dishonor. Honor

is a front for guilt,
therefore dishonor . . .

Something twists here,
a typical Greek lesson,

the writhing of a woman,
ten dead sheep. Enraged,

my son, without desiring it,
lays upon his sword, his name

spittle between consonants,
the luckless resonance

of blood. He wept, Homer says,
on a beach with good drainage

for what the heart
gives out, which is not

honor. He produces his lyre,
as usual. I consider the beach,

the rocks that cut my feet,
the smoking ash, the teeth

and fillings that make
enormous clatter after

and I ask: Homer, where
is honor? He pauses, pinches up

soot. Ajax, he says,
take off your helmet,

then he lets the specks
muddy the water.

Mother's Minotaur

If I follow her through the maze
where the goal is a god
I can't fail. But so rapt

in choice, or seeming choice,
we are caught by the dark
with the *chi, chi* of martens

in houses on poles, the airlines
blinking over. Turning away
in basement silence, we struggle off

our dresses, make a bed of hair,
fall asleep together. And when
the topiary shifts and she calls out,
I'm dreaming the snorting closer.

Epithalamion

Beyond that first domestic kiss
where we're all Odysseus,
the Mediterranean sways enigmatically.
But believe me, the depths scare

all the sailors. It is the cruise
to the vanishing point
where Scylla weds Charybdis
and the gulls cry Divorce!

where the faces you once admired
ghost up, only partly bodiless,
that makes you declare all love art.
Late at night, on deck,

the moon dims all prior scars
to mere regret because
even becalmed, the fish
throwing themselves

into the boat, the compass
too hot to consult, you must find
each other. You don't have
to go back, history's a lesson

no one's required to take over.
So what if the Cyclops rages,
wanting all your attention,
and Calypso's doing an odalisque

on the back deck—it's your ship,
the wind is good, and ardor
is all you need in place of weather,
the stays creaking forever.

Lithium

The fool laughs and weeps
and won't eat and the gods
like that—they dance
with the bear just to open
its belly. See, the gods

are just sons of the last gods.
The joke's that if a fool
wears out, another
cracks nuts behind
the curtain. Let this

frighten you, sister:
nothing's wrong until a god
crawls up your dress hissing
sick—if you catch him.
The gods love a fool.

The Smell of Burning Pennies

The red claw of rhubarb
presses out of the cold ground
and six cats, all something gray,
convene under the terrace for the dog.

It is time to look for gods
in the basement with the plumber
but even there it's like knocking
on the womb: Be a woman, and no answer.

Instead, under the sky's corridor
of planes, the dog puts back her ears
and the shadows disappear, all six.
The smell reminds me again:

Little one, count your coins
for the gods number them.
It is a votive pressing up from the earth,
something burning already.

Sketch Lesson

She can't draw an angel without soiling it, without
   lines, and she can't have one
      without pressing herself to the sketch
       yet its thousands

of what we call feathers—
     pardon the limited imagination—
   make her sneeze just thinking
about them, sneeze until pearls form
      from the irritation, wild ones,

like the moon

      in a big breath over Toledo
where she's sketching and necking, the second
   like swans grooming.

     And after
the pearl dissolves into the vinegar
      of night, and the lines of the sketch
drift off to blacken the path of
      however she got there,
   her bones will bear the impress,
the way she once had a tail and gills,
   and the angel will sigh, creased as a bat,
   and as unlikely.

Picnic

The birdcalls are louder than Route 9 traffic,
all lung, but you can't find them,
staring at the bottom rungs of a dead pine,
at the deciduous aching with blossom.
The calls may as well be friction over holes
in space, or all legend, the bewitched
fussing in the boughs for attention.
You deflect the ants from your path,
thinking how one could brush away success
like a harmless nuisance. And with your
friends—you tackle the main hill with
a twig—your success would linger, a sour dishrag,
the job over. In double dactyls now,
the birds, and an ant successfully
drags a chestnut. You're stuck

in the *Why bother?* Like fertilizer or
fairy dust, hope gets tracked across
the cleaned-up floor. All those fabulous
bird tales, vulture versus hawk, explain this.
You sit on a hollow log which sinks in decay.
Listen, what about enchantment? A red fox
matching last fall's foliage, pads by, then
caught by the smell of you, turns its head.
You both want to run but not together. You sing
"My Old Kentucky Home" low so he stops.
If he were shot, the killer would think
he was doing you a favor. Last year success
was superconductivity, it happened in space
where no one lived. The birds go quiet.
You hug the anomalous sandwich.

Fairies

Godlets, like Chihuahuas to the Doberman,
with the reputation of Edwardian cherubic
busywork: nuts, berries, cobbling, wishes,
lack the epiphanous scrutiny of our century.
Toward this, I submit:

the Neanderthal, nervous with difference,
furious with vermin competition, clubs them
to a dodo finish, leaving the elaborate
Hawaiian fence work, the English hedgerow houses,
the Maori middens, their bones mistaken

for TV dinners', as one of many species caught
short or too small. Or perhaps they were just
children in hiding, from whatever raving invader:
"I had to load my .38 to get the little ones,"
that, California, the extinction, the Indians'.

Fairies, protect me, the boy prays, instead of
to angels. Dancing Sinatra in the moonlight,
the survivors plot and revel and switch babies
so parents' abuses get explained away, away,
to the insect link, the flashing caddis fly

whose pool, jewel, cool rhymes with its jet
and green lattice whirring over rotten logs
where hide plenty, dragging swords and maggot
scarves. Shrinks reduce the dragon for easy
assimilation: sex versus civilization,

so fairies become our lost Id, imprinted
in one inarticulate moment under a chair,

belly down, all terror and desire.
But small is good on our collapsed planet,
anything chipsize gets applause—just not the defenseless.

Today, while we're not watching, they burst
from our sets, and cats quickly kill them,
or furniture polish—or sadness, hearing
the locusts three feet under the sealed asphalt
signal their own out-of-synch resurrection.

A Moo from a Can with a Cow on It

The last dolphin won't save us.
The bombs strapped to his back
sink him further. The turtles
never turn once they reach

the pavement. Some musk (creosote?)
drives them—like us
in the Toyota, our limbs withdrawn,
in line for the on-ramp?

You can get all the endangered
stuffed, in bright colors,
but the baby turns towards
the birds every time, rapt.

What will he turn to later?
Peck, peck, peck—a toy
that dips forever? A moo
from a can with a cow on it?

In Kansas the last moose
kneels to the hunter. There is
a sound when you twist the trophy
from the body. They think

it's not speech that separates us,
but foresight. Listen
as the kittens are pulled
from the teat to the toilet.

Unicorn

As men, to try the precious unicorn's horn,
Make of the powder a preservative circle,
And in it put a scorpion.
                                —John Webster,
                                The White Devil

A scorpion struts through the ring of powder
then dies.

In Britain, 300 years ago, the scorpion
            was certainly as rare
as the unicorn but its death
            proved the unicorn lived.
                    But had died, of course,

its horn being ground to powder
                    which is white like
            the "white" rhino's,

white like what the girl from Amsterdam's
            licking off her mirror,
and now the rhino's rare. We think the girl's alive.

Then too, men pondered over
            the bones of the triceratops,
                            labeling them
            the blasted dragon's
ears. And ground them for sex.

                    It's no wonder Mattel

77

turns out a pink synthetic-maned unicorn
to fetch the eight-year-old virgins,
our best specimens.

Or that it took Lincoln seven hours to die.
That is, the twenty surgeons
packed into the small dressing room could cut
as well as ours but had no drugs.

He was a rare man
to proclaim emancipation, even under pressure,
to free black from white
even if that's still a matter of myth.

Such is progress:
the scorpion rising on its many legs, coming to,

and the unicorn
spread before the roaring fire

where the Dutch girl lolls, empowdered.

Wait

The weeping willow touches both lush banks.
The river is tensed, writhing between weeds with
names like *touch-me-not,* and a brown bear with
weeping-willow-honey-desire, rank
with recent love, pulls down branches, his teeth
set. Bugs skate past, unperturbed by bear maw,
the slathered jaw, the palsied honeyed paw,
taking care when mating only to eat

the other's hindquarters. Bear skat's just
more rubble at the base of the weeping
willow to the weed-dotted bank, all husk
deciduous. Wait, there's a man calling
Styx! Styx! But the river is not a dog,
the tree hardly weeping, the hole all dug.

Four

Ptolemy's Rules for High School Reunions

1.

Réunion's an island in the Indian Ocean
where one cats the boat backward to avoid
hurricanes, thus docking is a bit surprising
and, though the ozone's bad at the equator,
there's the Jell-O salad effect, three
sailors together and a crunchy Weltschmerz arises,
talk of getting there and who was Scylla
and who was corrupted. Let us, on the ocean
of adolescence, be this one day crack sailors,
geeks just Greeks mispelled.

2.

Years of dyslexics reading Twain aloud,
shop stars spit-polishing side tables,
young Werthers wild in dark halls—why return?
As inexplicable as a lesson in magnetics,
I want to correct a lifelong ennui,
some buzzing misery. And those who don't?
Are they better adjusted? Or so cruelly scarred
one relived moment sends them over?
College reunions recommend only lost youth,
not the clouded patina of childhood.

3.

It was a year of assassinations
then closed colleges, the re-creation
of peace and love, what we knew
we had but had to realize. Who knew
who taped the obscene French drill?
Threw the shotput a foot short

of the principal's window? Got pregnant
and got out of it? See us smiling
in the yearbook, dumb as draftees
to the march ahead of us.

4.
I'd like a yearbook for every year, all of us
choosing between six poses, composing truths
to fit our faces. Not one would be blacked out
by hastily assembled quorums ruling on pranks
to do with fire, toilets aflame on Main Street.
I have a right to expect such tolerance,
the pranksters and the teachers
now both in business, each asking
the other Can I help you?

5.
I drive past the once-raw landscape,
clean of ungulates and packs of cats,
accordioned into lots bought by
the wisest families instead of
station wagons, now golf course or
condo heaven, land of father, mother,
and of how I didn't need them—not
like now, the concrete under my tires
as gouged as headstones, and cracks
in the get-rich-quick sewers.

6.
Twenty years! It's a mockery,
parental wisdom come too true.
We had the smarts to avoid this, we had
backflips and long kisses. Obviously
wrinkles lay folded in the hankies
we cried in. I'll stick to the shadows,

the lighting's better and shadows
bear no children, they grow taller
evenings but not in years, mark
after mark etching the kitchen closet.

7.
I have an hour, I take the Y
to what all adolescents require:
a large enough mirror, a body of water.
The ash of its bonfires, burnt sagebrush
and cigarette, still smells forbidden.
Its dam, once the world's largest,
lies now unranked, though its waters
cover a whole town where divers report
stop signs and rubber tires. At the edge
I feel a suction, the unlived lives.

8.
I've never crossed it. I've walked
sandbars almost to the middle
but no motorboat took me, plunging,
farther. A full hundred miles around,
as deep as four fathoms, the lake's
a biologist's *pot-au-feu,* full of huge fish
hoary with hooks. And what else? Once,
past midnight, in a bucket-seated
Barracuda, I glimpsed a double-backed
terror in the steamed-up mirror.

9.
I won't go. I'll keep my dinner deposit
and eat in a café overlooking the water
where the trout is securely frozen and the sunset's
just a shade of blusher to the oversize matron
who seats me. They don't allow reticence

at reunions. They will pick and find wounds,
they will salt them. The stars mildew,
the screen door behind the steak plates vibrates.
I could be anywhere, tasting pickles
in barrels—sour regret, but for this.

10.
Until what's accomplished so outweighs
envy they name a street for you,
you go to see the trees nod,
a grave *plié* of boughs, the leaves
to rise in acknowledgment so complete
you stop the car and sit.
You'll outgrow this febrile need.
But still you must grow toward light,
death's the unremembered, the lost
blue of any day, a lack of curiosity.

11.
Bucks approach the roadside, poised
to lunge at my car, pry open the hood
with their horns. I turn up the news.
The bucks, the wheat fields fly jagged against
the moon flinging its gold—ach! It could be
paper whirling up at my windshield.
Radio off, AC off, windows down,
nothing but the deer behind me, I go
for the past. On the rise the road turns black,
the car seems to mount stars.

12.
The school's mutated grotesquely,
an octopus of windowless brick bulging
into parking new-metered,
with a new football field

as overweaning as the mill levy.
Inside, machines of all kinds replace
books, and not just motherboards
but navigators and Cuisinarts and videos.
Read: English courses cause dropouts.
Maybe they turn out robots.

13.
The dead greet me, their names wreathed
in poor taste outside the entry.
At least they can't whisper like the teachers
heat-sealing my name tag. Still we kiss:
You haven't changed a bit. Lies spread
like sunscreen over a vacant pool.
Then a lady computer salesman breaks in,
insisting language go all acronym. I miss
the dead, their drag races, swooping Pipers,
angel dust, bullets in which chamber?

14.
Mortgage-livered bankers, housewives
turned city managers, gaggles of teachers
emanate the most unexpected contentment
from their too-tight ties and bird-flecked
shifts. I should embrace them. Instead, shaken,
I search for Roger, just divorced
and terribly drunk, homeless really,
living from one rig to another. I remember him
prayerful over a vial of sulfur,
an explosion, then laughter.

15.
I bump a Dantean apparition, a man
so ballooned I recognize only his eyes,
ones I'd stared into for many lost hours.

Now they dart as he describes
his Burger Boy, the one he works in,
will never own. His children?
The eyes disappear in a grin. He brags.
He whines. How can he expect more
from them when the lesson he gives
is less? Our tears make us blind.

16.
Only once in their lives, a five-year
window, do men deal with women.
These specimens shy as I slow-dance before them.
In Africa, I whisper, Men never
stop courting. Damn, says Roger,
In Kalamazoo they say it's the ladies.
Then I'm sad as some otherwise
utilitarian version of me
blazes with color, recircling the tables
in Roger's gleeful intimacy.

17.
The talk I've missed is Blast the spicks,
Nicaragua's already half hammer and sickle.
An ex–Viet vet shakes his head. He's just done
five to fifteen in the state pen
for moving heroin through Denver. Hell,
I think they got their ideology together.
But the brother of the dead corporal contradicts:
Put up the flag, the VFW's good for more
than dances, make those mothers clap—for that's
a Miss Wheat, not a Rice Queen in the kitchen.

18.
Also Sorghum and Beet, depending on the market,
long-stemmed, more bulbed now than then,

but no gray in the frozen chuff of hair
hanging to her shoulders. Recently split
from a salesman too flat-footed for service,
she eyes the vet. Here *behind bars* is where
you go when you can't get your order,
not the cooler, not where life screeches
it's over. Hey, honey, what stickers
you got pasted to your bumper?

19.
There's PRO-NUKE on three pickups in the lot.
Ten states turned down the chance to handle
this little run-off, boasts math whiz mother
of seven folding the year-embossed napkin
into her vinyl clutch. We'll get more jobs,
better education, maybe a junior college where
I can get on in. There's a lobby against it,
right here in town, someone's always balking.
She downs her nutcup in a single gulp, orders
another Collins. We'll make the best of it.

20.
Oh, Loris who posed in a flesh-colored swimsuit
on a carhood cruising Main, Loris, of beer bottle
breasts and reports written in peanut butter,
Loris, who occasioned impassioned principals
and banned dances, who fled pregnant
the day after graduation to Texas, some said,
or Alabama, with what dread would you view
this latest invitation to high school?
If out of accident you received it,
what intern or warden would read it?

21.

Pudgy, Karen knew enough to choose sex
over food; giggly, to perfect the teacher's
stern Again? lonely, not to let on. Before
her lover died under his jacked-up Chevy, before
she gave up the baby, even before she showed me
the Dirty Monkey, her cat eyes supported
some quivering emotion, some unquietness.
We promised each other we'd be nuns together.
I broke that twice and she married an undertaker.

22.

Ina, my nemesis, sidles over. I feel
the planets check out of orbit. We kiss.
I have a fantasy she'll turn to mist.
But when the air clears there's *So this
is Charlie,* my line to her spouse.
She's had so many TV spots she's
got to fly to Europe for a rest,
he comments, nipping his mustache
with his lip. She lists a bit. Only I know
how much is left of the girl I hissed.

23.

A photo's all we have of Mary Alice,
the girl with hickies made to match
the black eye, all her father left her with.
Other girls wore scarves, turtlenecks,
makeup to mask that love could hurt.
She looks defiant still, and so passionate.
Our halls condoned no public emotion:
only the Weejun tassle, the fixed flip—
in short, the irreducible existential fop:
cool, as she was not.

24.

Wealth's easier to make than to keep,
our parents tell us. We keep only
our sense of humor. How many yuppies
to change a lightbulb? One to estimate
the replacement, one to hold it while
the earth turns for him, and one
to do the merger. Out of punks, joggers,
gourmands, heavy-metal addicts, coke fiends
and aerobic nuts, yuppies prove the anomaly,
their absence noted like royalty.

25.

The farmers make a show of smiling
despite land values, sinking parity,
drought dust etching their new-wizened
faces. Along their culverts, sunflowers
rage and spin, along their mortgaged
gleaming "systems." I don't understand
them or their teenaged children,
those who hand out recipes for
their prize-winning Holsteins, so pretty
They'd make a good pair of bridesmaids.

26.

Bursting from their white, almost blue,
collars, the ex-football stars
are bald "where it counts," their jokes
brimming with bravado that still sound
unearned, unlike their counterparts,
the detectives on my block,
outlandishly squeezed into straining
suitcoats. But they're armed,
clearly all that's lacking for the salesman
who insists: Go ahead, hit me.

27.
If most average twenty hours of TV weekly,
plus movies, chances are New York's
more familiar than their own driveway,
yet, terrified, how they malign my chosen city.
I claim more people die of car wrecks
driving cross-country than in our shoot-outs,
yet secretly I wonder. All those shadows
without psyche, all those double-parked
limos, the neighborhood flunky. Do come visit.
No one bothers me when there's tourists.

28.
Isn't that nice? A poet. How
different. Who will say I knew it?
We shuffle. What kind? I answer:
Figurative, Elegiac, Portrait,
Corn-fed Pastoral. Rhyming or what?
These college graduates harbor no longing
for effervescence, or my malaise. I explain
to two in line for the bathroom: See the scarf
caught in the draft between the biggest
buildings? I try not to let it land.

29.
Speech, speech as per our able president,
Ken-doll-handsome in his letter jacket,
segueing Hanoi with Bethann's twins
as the Beach Boys croon from a propped up Walkman.
Did orchids on parents make us flower children?
Crowned royalty, the class captains and queens,
taught us more about values than Civics, beauty
than Art, a confusion of honesties that turned
slight defects crippling, minor talents major.
But that was their moment of blossom.

30.
We say tomorrow, something informal,
not a reunion, saving us the effort
of parting. Oh, around noon, we say,
stroking the fender. The beach—
that place past Allstate? As we nod,
styrofoam blizzards off a passing flatbed.
Pigs love it, one farmer insists,
closing his window. Get prepackaged
before they die. No one's mentioned
death yet, just who would come to our fortieth.

31.
I've drunk too much, I toss, I stand
on my bed to look at my shelf.
How many others sleep under china dolls,
and dried sweetheart bouquets,
the air as still as Nefertiti's?
I'd rather be at the Holiday
at some wild party with strange bathrooms
and machines that release ice all night,
but for the flowers laid on a parents' stone
a half mile from the Interstate.

32.
Once we cruised the cemetery,
lights off, girl geeks with boys,
top down though rain sizzled at the tires.
Reds wanted to stop somewhere special,
the freshest. An angel gleamed in the wet
as he unearthed his trumpet
from the trunk, breathed into it.
Then sweetly, so sweetly Linda cried,
he played taps. So far we'd lost
nothing for good but gas money.

33.
I fall asleep and dream of the steak
on the barbecue, its marble
and bone pointing to the five o'clock past,
and pep club pressure so great
I don't notice
a parent's desolation,
the authentic cocktail, the pipe
with its djinn of smoke,
the slippers—surely he had slippers—
and the chicken-killing Corgy who was shot.

34.
The next day at the beach a few still wear
bikinis but the rest, wide-bodied, huddle
over grills as if it were too cold to strip,
and hungover men wrestle with grown offspring,
melancholy about almost losing. Middle age
revolts us. Better youth's revolt, I think.
Except for those epiphanous turns when divorce
is declared or late pregnancy rears, we're stuck
in our lives like wet clothes which
we would change if we had others.

35.
The lake seems larger, wringing shores
so far in the distance birds get lost
and islands sink as we watch. We need a ferry,
a blowup float that doesn't leak.
Sharon, gorging on Fritos, paddles it, belly-down.
You know about Elmo and the morning glory?
(Elmo was our cop and the flower was this funnel
for water control.) Well, he fell in, chasing drunks.
When they found him, his hair'd turned white.
I shiver. The far bank's that much closer.

36.
We discover a dinosaur's femur
below the washout, the bone veiled
in the *au jus* of the lake surf.
At some point, someone calls State Fish
and Game but waiting, we can't resist picking.
To hold back we go all elegiac, that is,
until Roger says Size? That don't mean nothing.
We ladies burst into laughter, sex our one discovery.
Yes, Arcadia's over for us—and our children,
the one location music videos aren't using.

37.
Next Time We'll Be Even Better
reads the ant-loved lime sheetcake.
As it's eaten, the squib improves:
Next We'll Be. Then, finally, Time. We part
if not Velcro noisy, not Teflon easy,
towels billowing as sleepy husbands
wrestle squalling children into seat belts,
those who wouldn't play together
despite the photos, the eternal misnomer:
They're your age and share your interests.

38.
We've circumnavigated ourselves—how often?
fixing the boat on stars that turn around
our turning. It's a no deposit, no return life,
a litter you never have to pick up
or admire. We care, we despair,
answers blare from *MacNeil/Lehrer*.
Old age hasn't set in, despite
obesity, alcohol, lack of charity.
We're pulling on the oars,
goddamit, and it's no short story.

39.
Villagers grow old together while we,
in modern diaspora, have only
our own arched eyebrows in the mirror,
no real peer to peer into.
We fear age's change, yet crave:
We're here! Odysseus returned.
But *disguised* as an old man?
We know better. Are Ptolemy's
wrinkles from staring at planets?
Or just a double-feature watcher's?

40.
Ptolemy, perched on his wacked-out stool
in some nightspot of the stars
dishes out his end-of-shtick: So what if
you're not the center of the universe—
with Einstein you can have it all:
Time and Space, stretched like spandex over
the Sirens Contentment. Listen while
they wail their punk lines, Girls who just want
fun and Honey, it's your life. The trip
is all there is. Lash tight.

Five

Public Works

How, in summer, a man and woman,
as in Paris, embrace under trees,
and the leaves and the grass
bend back and sweat

amends them, in a park where
the squirrels eat well, where
the bronze horse could heave off
its officer. How it is like water,

sex in summer. You cover
yourself, your leaves rippling,
the sun inside. In Calcutta,
Omdurman, even Paris, the bent

grass curls and dies and birds
take it away until slums root,
the trees bare in smooth hard lust.
Touching a man there as if no one

but the exiles espaliered
to the bare walls watch,
just the occasional touch. How,
at the far end another bronze

beckons, her robes folded over
children and jugs of water,
and Haitians pass her by, hands clasped,
walking home into

the dark. How the roundness
of their faces shine as leaves, not money.
How, when the general dismounts,
swords fall from the arches,

speeches sigh from the trees,
and his first words to her
are what's carved in
by the ghostlike, love-struck loiterers.

Sex

I hear you on the ladder stirring in the eaves
in that blind way of last night, searching
the end by feel. Two hawks cross in the mirror
behind me as I listen, a foot from breakfast.
What a complicated thing, the neatly intersected.
Then the ladder eases down with its smell of cut pine
years after some machine made it whole,
bearing fresh wilderness at every opening.

Left-handed Women

You see far over his shoulder, past the sloppy moon
and the argyle fall lawn. You see how his hands, suddenly
brusque on the small of your back, try to sculpt your flesh.
Yet you don't see, the light is always failing under his touch,
the nape needs its slight kiss, the important lid. It's what's
been withheld a decade from the mother that searches your
    curves,

that says *Precious,* it's your sleeping self, warmed to life
in the bird-heavy air. But soon there's more current,

a series of buried brightnesses on a solemn night
where cars honk by accident, and the strength of that caress
eventually reveals otherness. It seems
one of you must yield. All those role models damning biology
were never girls. The promise is: pain, then more mature
    pleasure.

Thus the moon moans, the desparate worm advances with no
    terror
whatsoever. Grow up, grow—
then it's over, the pleasure grazing, not this species-sure
exhalation that lies beside you, so suddenly separate.
If this be adult, the effort's mawkish. You are the one
bearing the darkened corner where the embrace, so tight then
to your slick swollenness, could have begun in earnest.
Later you find some less willful match, yourself perhaps,
and being car handy, you understand how you could get more
than he does, and that covers the logic of it,
the larger share, the Chevy turning over and over.

To Autumn

Like talc, the white ash with its fruity scent
    settled on my pep club sweater until
Dad threw in so many bales the fire went
    out in the incinerator and Bill,
the sheriff, sprayed gas on it. In the blaze,
    I saw him guffaw, the spooked prairie gust
        having shifted, smothering his workday
    hack, the grin maybe for his first real bust
but more likely from what he was inhaling.
That Dad, prosecutor of the whole region,
    should provide me my first real brush with drugs

bore evidence of our innocence. Things
    were cool—I brought kitchen leavings to heave
and heaved with them my blank smug cheerleading
    demeanor while these humbugs-in-shirtsleeves,
eyes watering, pointed at the stars
    as if they were lineups of TV minions,
        and ignored me. Far off, the souped-up cars
    of this fall's birthdays tore past on quick dares,
waking dogs and babies, circling Kildare's
where, on good nights, you could pass for eighteen
    until the cops came. This haul was not theirs

but the Interstate's, where hapless, blonde, jean-
    clad college students turned on and made cash
for school. At least that's what they pled, sixteen
    days later, according to the rehash
in the newspaper. By then all the leaves
    had turned and a wash of smoke had faded
        the small town back to relative order,

and the stubblefields had been burnt to give
the corn room, with me out in the roadbed
where the rabbits cowered as the fire spread,
sniffing what grew on the perimeter.

Brassiere: Prison or Showcase?

Great breasts! whispers the décolletéd clerk
of the old gray lady hugging a negligee.
So French, her suggestion the woman
had nothing to do with them and thus

was more worthy. How naturally we take to
the twinning of marriage, two breasts
on the beast Lust. Only after ten years
do I learn you can't pee for tests, a graphic

restatement of your body's Otherness. Mother
kept on cooking after she called Dinner
and I often ate cindered burgers, annealed noodles,
my last lesson in nursing, separation.

No, there's not much play in those blind boobs,
those double poets reinventing Elephant.
Your penis bobs Yes, no answer. In Darwin's
theory, individuals aren't accountable

for their bodies, the gray lady's
only flotsam in Sex's bath. But dear,
don't cinch the bra tight to make us produce.
That's outré, Lamarckian.

A Scarlet Bird

They are preparing aphrodisiacs for lunch
while I drink white wine, adrift
under the moss-hung oaks and bougainvillea
blooming thick as genitals, and drifting
away from you, a thousand miles north.

A scarlet bird wants to eat from my hand.
Its feet are two tweezers plying my flesh
as if searching for slivers. I too

am hungry, picking at promises like a sailor
calling out depths and this drink confuses me
with its single, lonely message: one throat,
one belly, one heart quickening with alcohol
and warming. All I have to do is reach out

and I can eat the bird, even its feathers.

Xmas House

Could I plunge my ballpoint into
your throat the moment you purple—
       even then? Make a gaping hole
for air where the syllable catches? If we
           invented whipped cream
and its cannister to deplete the ozoned air,
       that suicidal turn, what about
a gingerbread beam to block it?

       You breathe gingerly, Heimlich bruised,
       and the boy under the tree
       points the cannister down his throat
and misses, the spray
           making a kind of white beard.
It's for him you are saved,
           and the house. I grab

the one throwing himself over the edge
       of the carriage, who does an etrechat
being lifted, whose syllable is *la*
         after forced feeding.
As the dog takes food pellet by pellet
       to the carpet and swallows,
          we forget how brave the baby is.

Dog/God

As the shrink's often as confused
as the patient, dyslexia is impossible
to spell, the "y" and "i" Greek logic.

A boy's left guessing—few girls—
which door's left and which right
and when Humiliation roars out

the clock hands spin, and he hides again.
Come out, the mother calls, come out.
You'll be da Vinci yet and no jailbird

cutting words from a newspaper
to better the ransom letter.
But the words won't stay on the line,

every letter scrambles, gestalt's
the only way he gets it, *dog*
seems right for so long.

In our savannah or swamp of origin,
did the track or the animal come first?
Homo dyslexia shrugs, outlines the bison

better than any of the others remember.
Shaman? The millenium carries the chromosome.
Still, it's a life of *whatchamacallit,*

the devil jiggling the A for apple
while he stares at it, and everyone else
is already so terribly sorry.

On That Day

Your father will not be home.
You and I will fill the sinks,
pull the files against the door,
count the cans of food. And when

he knocks and calls out,
we'll shout Go *away*.
Will you understand?
I'll have no words for it,

nor for the glow pulsing through
the walls like a flashlight
in the mouth, nor for the windows
that break from sound you can see.

But for once we will have lots
of time for stories: how it was,
how it might have been. Eventually,
I will put my breast to you

no matter what age you are,
hoping you can make it run.
It will be the whole of the world
I have left, that horizon.

A Cure for Hiccups

Every time the door opens,
the mother bird flies off. What's left
slumps and pulses. I determine
it will live,
"house finch" in the book,
practiced at distraction, the mother
always laying on lintels,
the others, unhatched,
just bad luck. "Mrs. Micawber

was never seen without one or the other
taking nourishment," wrote Dickens. Twins, nursing.
And if the bird can't deliver extra lunches?
I have only one door.

Perhaps the other eggs hold in
the mother's heat. I turn off
the porch light each dawn
to watch the daylilies open to their one day,
and the baby, ending sleep
with hiccups.
I try to stare him into being, just as,
in Emergency, they gave me
those small shoes
to look at.

Death for Franchise

I've read that poem: usually
a bird comes crashing into a window, then
       there's an afternoon of sighs.
                              This time
I'm talking ten years, and as much denial
       as fits a shrink's datebook. Wake up,
              they say, but wakes
are depressing in any direction—
                     what about a nice birthday,
       candles lit in darkness celebrating
a something, if not a life.
              So what if I forget it's exciting,
this race to kiss death's backside,
                     especially if someone else has already
       died "in advance."
The pot metal angel growing up out of the sod,
       doesn't fool anyone. Plato isn't
              out there, bouncing baskets
off a hoop with my son's grown friends,
                     and the dog is new.

Rogue Transmissions

"What is it you see
From up there always—"
—Frost, "Home Burial"

At daylight, the air sinuous
with smoke, I left candle stubs
or their puddled wax
in *pensione* ashtrays. There were always
more candles in cathedrals,
all those cold cathedrals.

Religions wasn't why.
Insomnia wasn't why.
Setting out candles in empty bottles
drunk to make me drunk,
I earned my comfort,
the flame burning in my eyes until it burnt my eyes.

But what fades, flares.

Now I turn on the TV and its attendant machine,
hoping the past on tape is just the past,
the way people in a landscape never see it change.
What begins is a perfect fall day, though
at the time such perfection's not noted,
looking into the camera, saying our names.

It's the same park, a different, dead child,
exactly the age of the one watching,
but one with a beauty I'd forgotten,
ascribing it to all children of a certain size,

color eyes. Then I lose the frame,
there's our feet, the sky. In Borges's story

the initiate convinces the diviner
he has visions by sharing them.
This tape's just light
in numbered bundles, not marble,
something to crack my head against.
Yet I stare into that cold screen, I do stare.

All Happy Families

The fields are frozen, swart rows banded white
with ribbons of ice, each a horizon
planted with a sun. The station wagon's
old back end takes the ruts shocklessly, waking
everyone, even the potential son-
in-law whose carousing late last night
merited a bowed-head-in-hands. The light
scissoring at him, however, is not
unexpected. "If Dad can find a spot,

we always skate Christmas morning," she told
him at 2 A.M., her lips grazing his.
Still, he couldn't believe it, six siblings,
gallons of chili, chocolate, ice cold
garlic bread in aluminum wrapping
glittering on the moon terrain of bright
broken ice. Midnight, over the vast bowl
of punch, its deliquescing strawberries,
he sensed these vagaries of family life.

A coon rattles cornstalks, a grouse grouses.
Breathless as the fixed fish below, solemn
as he is heavy, Dad proclaims the ice
solid. Scraping over the ripples, his skates
grate, turn and then upend. Everyone feels
for their bones, then everyone eats and waits
for the sun to come out again, one gold
medal that changes nothing. They sing. Wind
whips their ankles, the youngest circling

still, cheeks as ruddy as any Hummel.
It is to him that the son-in-law skates, ·
wobbly, done with the querulous adults.
Stopping, he shaves ice. "I'll bet you can't skate
backwards," the runt bellows. The family turns.
Backwards he inscribes a heart against a crack
of ice so the crack becomes the arrow
roiling love, whatever they take that for.
Noon looms. No one wants to skate anymore.

"Don't bleed on me." "You're crushing my glasses."
"Stop dragging in Chaucer." "Is it true that
the Ik stole food even from their children?"
"You would remember that." They all laugh. As
for their tipsy mother, in a red hat
at the punch bowl, they try to forget that
as best they can the day after. They love
her embarrassing them, the attention.
"There's still hope. Maybe she'll like grandchildren."

"Sleep with me, come on—you know what I mean."
He doesn't hear the caterwaul upstairs,
the dishwasher overflowing, the child
falling. She's a nice girl, that's the problem,
that's why he likes her. "We're getting nowhere.
O.K. Let's just go through the motions, them
motions." He rolls off. "Caesar's who got
Cleopatra pregnant, wasn't it? Or
was it Alexander?" "Shshshsh, it's father."

His bear-shamble invades the dark bedroom.
Skates glitter under his arm, just sharpened.
He reaches for the light in the closet.
"Ahem. I didn't know just where to put them."
There's a swallowing, a gainful open-

ended silence as the skate edges ruin
the carpeted closet floor. "The fire's lit
upstairs, if you want it." He doesn't smile
or hides it, the joke's on them. In a while

they won't remember that earnest stirring,
what animal hurry got them so tight
no strawberry punch could assuage it.
Dad sighs, passing portraits. It's so complex.
The kid—he's thirty-eight?—no doubt has been
around, he knows what he's getting into.
Life, that's enough. Wait till I tell Mother.
She's smarter than me about secret sex,
the frozen pond, post-coital regret.

II.

Almost twenty years since she attempted
such silliness. She usually sat it
out, freezing. Now her fiancé wings by,
the wind pushing him forward so he looks
borne aloft. Her frame of mind exactly.
Two sisters windmill just behind him, book-
happy, but unmarried too. We tend to
mate late, that's what the shrink said. We're busy
earlier. She skates to where the ice goes

thin, where weed stalks pierce the transparent lace
and air bubbles form pockets for crickets
that scarcely breathe, and maybe fish. She could
get through here, melt it with just her breath,
or break it stomping. Just like her family,
frozen under her skin, the chromosomes
free like ions but the glands taped shut—by
too much religion in the overbearing
hasenpfeffer that is her family,

that kissed crucifix? Finally she can hear
them quarreling, so verboten before.
Aqua and orange, the two colors she likes
best, perfect for a good Bohemian
bride. You're too old, hisses Persephone.
The next gust sets the last grain shivering.
The BVM? No. She blinks. Couldn't be.
The old sty-song of femininity
linked forever with rank fecundity.

He skates out a heart with their names inside.
She blushes, applauds. So old and eggless
she'll make the sacrifice, pick up the socks,

twice a week eat compromise, for writing
up writs she's done in plaid before, for less
reward, nothing but money. Some garlic's
lodged in her molar. Good luck? The grain spins
to gold even in this light. Oh, let's love
before Persephone pulls off those gloves.

She can't believe she thought that, especially
about the socks. She passes him after
he nearly cuts down her sister, not that
May doesn't deserve it, dallying, hat
waving as if for a bull. She giggles.
It gets her in the knees, she nearly falls
over. What if she took lessons? In ardor,
she means, who could teach her to deal with males
safely? The shrink says keep trying, fail.

What, Persephone? Promise you a snake
to stand on, something phallic yet gelid?
O.K. We'll see if you're squeamish. Too old, the wind
moans. A pheasant starts, its wings beating wild
like an overtaxed heart. She's hushed as air.
What of wire-cupped breasts, the dragging derriere?
She unlaces her skates, he tousles her hair.
Persephone sinks underground. If you look
long enough, it's snowing. She goes to cook.

An hour late. The fire's out of control
as usual, the chili's burnt, mother's
tearful, scalded by chocolate, and chaff
floats in everything. No trouble at all
they all lie. We're really quite happy, Mom.
And the youngest does a half-pirouette
to console her, landing, spread-eagle, on
someone else's anatomy, stooges
all. "You're not children," she snaps and rouges

118

her cheeks even there, against the crisp wind,
then lights a cigarette, the box warning-
side-down. "Just because you were born here years
ago doesn't mean you can regress when
you visit. I love you but you spook me.
Get up a game of bridge, you vidiots,
I didn't raise you on crazy-eights. One
hand and you'll beg to suck your thumb again.
And get the affianced a scotch, women."

III.

A whisker in the cow flop, a sorghum
shoot fluttering against the pellucid
snow, the wavy dusklight deny the ice
that penetrates deep into the dried dung
to bug level, where it's egg-tight, white-rice-
blind, and nothing moves. The pond's slick grid
goes black until the stars relight the scoring.
There'll be a web then, running its faint lines

in aching circlings, and intersections
of collision. The windmill turns, water
pumps under the frozen surface but cows
still die of thirst unless the ice is broken.
A couple of coyotes that sound like wolves
to people from the city circle or
stop, ears up. The skaters turn in their beds
or bed as crazy-eight infinities
cut through them, a cool blade blood-embroidered.

The Root of Father Is Fat

Cry uncle!
but you mean Dad.
He grunts where you've socked his gut.
Post-war, he says, men flocked to a pool
said to dissolve fat.
But not me.
Got to have a drum in front.
Go ahead, hit me again.

The ease in the middle
lets in air between the bottom
buttons. But lean?
That's another clef
on the bacon strip. He bends over
with Atlas arms
to show you legs
upsidedown against a wall, to show you
veins.
Cream's good for clearing
the throat, he says. Mmmmmmmmmmm.
Then you can sing Sinatra.

Appomattox

That's me, arguing for another effort,
not enough signatures. One of the other me's
      insinuates and squanders breath on Thanks. Thanks
for the fight he says with his big Dad body
      like the others were boys.

                   But we are all
boys fascinated with fighting. Uncle! Uncle!
      breaks out until we are not arguing,
            we are nodding and signing
and the horses, waiting like women
with eyes down,
         scrape at the earth underfoot.

Should they shoot the horses too? They want to know.
      Or put dirty holes in the white flag?
           We have to let them cartoon in
          Michaelangelo putting the reach on god
because we can't see the whole picture,
      we don't have the aerials and besides,
they say, Let that be a lesson.

And who are the they but two parents
      silhouetted in the front seat
         by oncoming traffic,
    and on their radio is some tune
sung along by the very back,
         traitors, all shrill brothers?

Pulling Up Mint Accidentally

You're so close to the sky, all your atoms
feel holes they are kin to, and eagles could snatch
        up the spread.

              You swallow Hey!
        and start. The bread's too dry as always,
and the stream's so noisy
        you don't hear the bottles emptying.

                    Dizzy,
you make sandwiches, something over and under,
     protective, and the savage teethmarks
           in the sausage do not trouble
      the gatherer who's just
pulled up mint accidentally.

               A picnic resonance
sets in,
      as if Father had carried the basket,
      as if you could see his muscles, as if
he had come, as if

           the wind devil,
smearing the field below with perspective,
      is already
      flipping the spare light plates,
all that negative space, high.

How He Grew

Sentiment hovers
around the brutish fur of what was once
stuffed but never alive, its likeness not bear
but less, to appeal to parents. That
     is the sentimental part:
the child's self left out,
     the teeth and sex.

     His report notes progress
in social exchange.
     You watch same
flutter, extinguish.
         He's such a sweet—
the telltale teeth marks.
     You want to see yourself repeated?
Woe to him who would have wants
and refuse to play.
He is sick, they say.
Bite back, you.

     Now you walk toward him. He retreats:
sex the forcefield. He has his hands
that are yours in front of him,
     and what you see is—
     a strong man, bulging,
holding up the wall.

     He goes away to camp
so long you're not hoping
to catch sight of yourself and then
     you do—your own sullenness,

         wounds made flesh. You want
to eat him, take his limbs and—
                  It's that fierce.
But you close your mouth
and come away with fur of the most
         synthetic.
         And this is kind.

The Septic Conversation

Did I mention the way water
                charts a slope across the gravel?
If not, please note. And let me suggest
                taking that south fork, for
all judgment lies with the water. That is,
shelter rises from the brink of totem,
                that is, a home on a slope is trouble.

        Take the gravel encroaching bedside.
On the south fork, which is to say,
                the one with proximity to the kitchen,
water is truth, and gravel lies. A clean fork
is what you have a shelter for,
                not the housewife standing at the sink
with its little slope, rinsing remains.

Such totem. See how one
        is atop the other—number one wife,
           number two, then children?
                It is like
                    water

                water
that does not resist like gravel, the way
        gravel at the bottom of a bed gathers.
So please find water to clean whatever's
        caught in the filter. Then stop to
           hear her speak.
      She speaks.

Inventor

The jay streaks through the lilacs
     in color clash.
I note down: *Invent*
    outdoor birdswing
          so birds drunk
on berries fall off in plaid
    in front of my window.
          I file it. After all,

the pussy willow's barely tufted—
          I have time.
    At the drain, lifting its feet,
      a Modigliani bird—another invention?
The brook agrees
    so brookishly, gulping at runoff
      like a bear in spring,
    like my husband. He didn't trust my patents:

      the gutter chain
        the collapsing arthritic's cane
      a lever for pulling old stumps
         in heavy rain

But every act harbors a corresponding gadget.

        It is that way with God:
adjusting the acorn, locking the tree.
    With the womb, He was clearly Italianate,
the bulbous lines, the excess.
    I often think of Him
      humming Beatles songs like me, over
        six Mason jars of improved pickling—

my offspring?
          The dog laughs. You heard it:
a choke, then black gums, a frothing irony.
          He's all wet from rescuing bones
                    from the brook. He drops them in,
                              then goes in after.
          The brook's rising with bones and I'm afraid
          the electricity will fail. Will the dog

                    save me with his laughing?
                    That's what this invention's for:
          the automatic rosebush waterer,
                    hooked to the sun and this wheel,
          in perpetuity. Once a pirate working
                    on my outboard told me, Betty, better sand
trickling in the hourglass than a shifting dune.
                    Even the Sudanese
plant borders of aloe against the drifts.
          Besides I like the look of roses.

          Oh, that's the husband at the door, scratching.
Nights his furry self stands naked
                    before me, until the dog
removes his stuffing.
                              O bear! Only by opening
          the blinds do I see he's bleeding.
          But it's me, not him, aching
                    with overdue maternity,
the inventor.
                    A simple drawerful of cobwebs
          kept for emergency does for him,
                    self-sticking,
                              then together we apprise
                              the chimney,
          holding hands and chatting about the soot stains.

That was in winter before he died, the deft
        air stealing all we were speaking.

                  Yesterday
      a patent came for my speech retrieval unit,
an unusual event, even for me, because
     the government usually can't get
past the drawings. And these were intricate:
        I had the duck by the neck, her feet
         in food coloring, each step
     inked in. It all made sense—listen
to the ducks now. And just in time for the aspect—
        ghosts are aspects, aren't they?
Of all but speech I have memory,
        that one sense shy of mimicry.

    In the spring, now, in fact,
I take the blackfly larvae off rocks
              in the rapids.
    On toast, pre-maggot, the very eggs
     of mortality, eating them I figure
I can lure Death itself, a raccoon
washing and washing in the dark,
     and from there, patent the trap.
I'll be rich if it works.
    Works, go the frogs, *works, works.*

Terese Svoboda is the author of *Cannibal, Laughing Africa, All Aberration* (Georgia, 1985), and *Cleaned the Crocodile's Teeth*. Her honors include the Bobst Award for Fiction, the Iowa Poetry Prize, and the Lucille Medwick Award and Cecil Hemley Award, both from the Poetry Society of America. Svoboda resides in Hawaii and New York.

The Contemporary Poetry Series

EDITED BY PAUL ZIMMER

Dannie Abse, *One-Legged on Ice*
Susan Astor, *Dame*
Gerald Barrax, *An Audience of One*
Tony Connor, *New and Selected Poems*
Franz Douskey, *Rowing Across the Dark*
Lynn Emanuel, *Hotel Fiesta*
John Engels, *Vivaldi in Early Fall*
John Engels, *Weather-Fear: New and Selected Poems, 1958–1982*
Brendan Galvin, *Atlantic Flyway*
Brendan Galvin, *Winter Oysters*
Michael Heffernan, *The Cry of Oliver Hardy*
Michael Heffernan, *To the Wreakers of Havoc*
Conrad Hilberry, *The Moon Seen as a Slice of Pineapple*
X. J. Kennedy, *Cross Ties*
Caroline Knox, *The House Party*
Gary Margolis, *The Day We Still Stand Here*
Michael Pettit, *American Light*
Bin Ramke, *White Monkeys*
J. W. Rivers, *Proud and on My Feet*
Laurie Sheck, *Amaranth*
Myra Sklarew, *The Science of Goodbyes*
Marcia Southwick, *The Night Won't Save Anyone*
Mary Swander, *Succession*
Bruce Weigl, *The Monkey Wars*
Paul Zarzyski, *The Make-Up of Ice*

The Contemporary Poetry Series

EDITED BY BIN RAMKE